D1275695

Our Environment

Biofuels

Karen D. Povey

KIDHAVEN PRESS

An imprint of Thomson Gale, a part of The Thomson Corporation

THOMSON

GALE

Detroit • New York • San Francisco • San Diego • New Haven, Conn. • Waterville, Maine • London • Munich

For more information, contact
KidHaven Press
27500 Drake Rd.
Farmington Hills, MI 48331-3535
Or you can visit our Internet site at http://www.gale.com

Picture Credits:
Cover: © Marcos Brindicci/SYGMA CORBIS; © Salem Krieger/ZUMA/CORBIS, 17; © Bob Sacha/CORBIS, 11; © George Steinmetz/CORBIS, 7; © Paulo Whitaker/CORBIS, 29; Mario Anzuoni/Reuters/Landov, 39; Marcos Brindicci/Reuters/Landov., 14; Al Golub/Reuters/Landov, 21; Zainal Abd Halim/Reuters/Landov, 31; Daniel Laclair/Reuters/Landov, 15; David Molzinarishvili/Reuters/Landov, 37; Reuters/China News photo/Landov, 40; Munish Sharma/Reuters/Landov, 34; Neal Ulevich/Bloomberg News/Landov, 18; Steve Zmina, 5, 8, 24, 25, 26, 27

LIBRARY OF CONGRESS CATALOGING-IN-PUBLICATION DATA

Povey, Karen D., 1962–
  Biofuels / by Karen D. Povey.
    p. cm. — (Our environment)
  Includes bibliographical references and index.
  ISBN 0-7377-3560-0 (hard cover : alk. paper) 1. Biomass energy—Juvenile literature. I. Title. II. Series.
  TP339.P68 2006
  333.95'39—dc22

2006011597

Printed in the United States of America

contents

chapter one

Energy and the Environment

Every day, billions of people around the world rely on energy to maintain healthy and comfortable lives. Energy allows people to cook food, get water, and heat their homes. Energy powers computers, provides hot showers, and keeps food and drinks cool in the refrigerator. Energy connects people and products all over the world through car, truck, train, and airplane travel.

The energy the world demands comes at a heavy cost to the environment, however. Producing fuel to create energy can have harmful effects on land, air, water, and wildlife. Using energy causes pollution, changes weather patterns around the world, and even harms human health.

Fossil Fuels

Most of the energy that powers the activities of daily life is produced through the burning of **fossil fuels**. Fossil fuels were formed millions of years ago as plants and animals died and were buried under

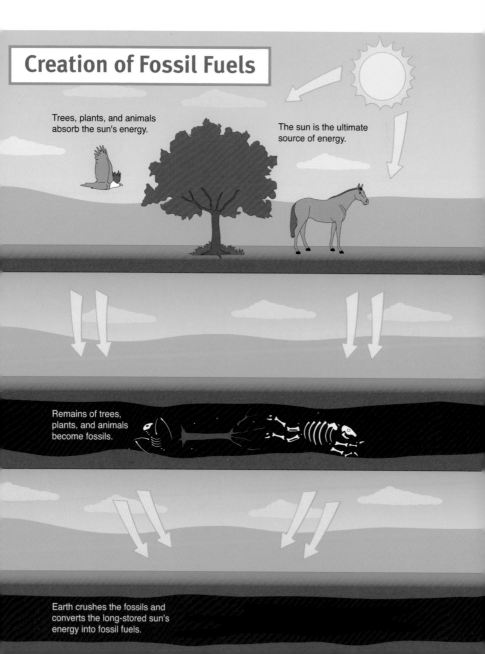

Creation of Fossil Fuels

Trees, plants, and animals absorb the sun's energy.

The sun is the ultimate source of energy.

Remains of trees, plants, and animals become fossils.

Earth crushes the fossils and converts the long-stored sun's energy into fossil fuels.

layers of soil and rock. The weight of these layers created great pressure and heat that acted on the plant and animal remains. Over time, this process caused chemical changes to take place in the remains, turning them into fossil fuels.

There are three types of fossil fuels. The most commonly used is petroleum, also known as oil. Petroleum supplies about 40 percent of all the world's energy needs. Petroleum is used to make the gasoline and diesel fuel that powers cars, trucks, and airplanes. Another fossil fuel is coal, which provides about 24 percent of the world's energy. Coal is used mostly to fuel power plants that create electricity for homes, businesses, and factories. The third type of fossil fuel is natural gas. It provides about 22 percent of the world's energy and is used mainly as a fuel for heating homes and cooking food.

Reaching Fossil Fuels

To obtain fossil fuels to use for energy, geologists must locate the oil, coal, and gas underground. Then it must be removed. Harvesting the fuel deposits that lie far beneath the earth can have serious effects on the environment. Coal is removed by digging mines that extend deep underground or by digging enormous pits on the surface of the earth. During mining, huge amounts of soil and rock must be removed to reach the coal below. For every ton of coal mined, 25 tons of excess rock and dirt are also

A blackened pit remains after coal has been stripped from the Earth's surface.

removed. Many mines cause serious pollution when rainwater washes over discarded rocks containing fragments of coal. The rainwater carries harmful chemicals into soil, streams, and lakes.

Removing petroleum and natural gas from the ground also poses environmental risks. Oil and natural gas are pumped from deep wells drilled into the ground and land on at sea. Modern drilling techniques provide many safeguards to keep oil from spilling from the wells. However, spills still occasionally take place. Transporting the oil through pipelines and on tanker ships can also be hazardous to the environment. Pipelines can leak or break. Oil tankers can have accidents, spilling huge quantities of oil onto the land or into the sea.

Oil is highly toxic, or poisonous, and can remain in water and soil for a long time after it is spilled. In 1989, the *Exxon Valdez* oil tanker ran onto rocks in Alaska's Prince William Sound. The 11 million gallons (42 million liters) of oil that seeped from its hull killed thousands of sea otters, seabirds, and other marine animals. Some scientists predict that the spill's harmful effects on wildlife may last for decades.

Burning Fossil Fuels

Although harvesting and transporting fossil fuels may sometimes damage the environment, the greatest harm comes when these fuels are used to provide energy. When burned in car and factory engines, fossil fuels release a poisonous mix of chemicals such as carbon monoxide and nitrogen oxide into the air. Some of this pollution can be seen in the form of dirty smog that hangs over cities. Pollution causes breathing problems such as asthma and contributes to birth defects.

Another type of pollution caused by the burning of fossil fuels is **acid rain**. Acid rain is formed when chemicals such as sulfur and nitrogen from burning coal and car exhaust react with oxygen and water in the atmosphere. This reaction forms

The Greenhouse Effect

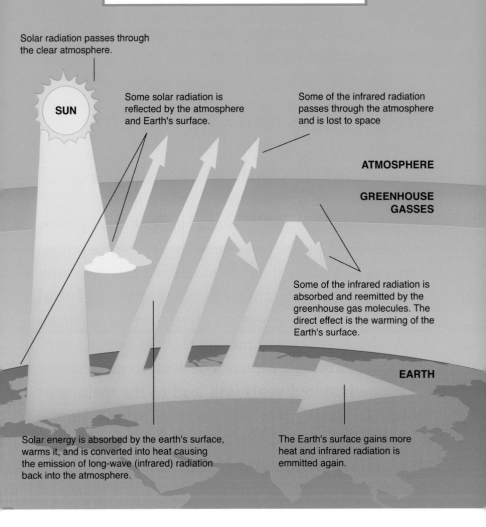

Solar radiation passes through the clear atmosphere.

SUN

Some solar radiation is reflected by the atmosphere and Earth's surface.

Some of the infrared radiation passes through the atmosphere and is lost to space

ATMOSPHERE

GREENHOUSE GASSES

Some of the infrared radiation is absorbed and reemitted by the greenhouse gas molecules. The direct effect is the warming of the Earth's surface.

EARTH

Solar energy is absorbed by the earth's surface, warms it, and is converted into heat causing the emission of long-wave (infrared) radiation back into the atmosphere.

The Earth's surface gains more heat and infrared radiation is emmitted again.

toxic chemical compounds that may be carried long distances by the wind. Eventually these chemicals fall to the ground in rain or snow. Acid rain kills trees as well as plants and animals living in lakes and streams. Acid rain has affected large areas of forest in Canada, the northeastern United States, Europe, and Asia. In China, where the use of coal-produced energy is growing rapidly, nearly

40 percent of forests and farmlands have been badly damaged by acid rain.

Fossil Fuels and Climate Change

Besides creating pollution, chemicals released by the burning of fossil fuels are thought to be affecting the climate of the earth. These chemicals, such as carbon dioxide, are known as **greenhouse gases**. Greenhouse gases trap heat in the atmosphere, causing a gradual rise in the earth's temperature. Scientists believe that over time, this **global warming** will have serious effects on the environment. Many scientists predict that an average temperature increase of even a few degrees over the next one hundred years will lead to the melting of polar ice, raising sea levels and increasing storms and droughts. Global warming may also lead to the extinction of many plant and animal species.

The Demand for Fossil Fuels

The environmental problems caused by fuels are expected to worsen as energy use around the world increases. It is estimated that by 2035, the world will use twice the energy that it does today. Currently, the greatest demand for energy is in Europe, Japan, and the United States. In fact, the United States, home to only 4.5 percent of the world's population, uses about 25 percent of the world's total energy. It

China is building hundreds of power plants like this one to satisfy its energy needs.

also produces about 25 percent of the carbon dioxide that contributes to global warming.

Other parts of the world are expected to soon catch up to the energy use of the United States. Many developing nations have fast-growing economies with rapidly increasing demands for energy to fuel factories and provide the comforts of modern life to their citizens. For example, the demand for electricity in Chinese homes has quadrupled since 1996 as more people can afford to buy televisions, air conditioners, and refrigerators. The Chinese government expects to build sixty power plants each year for the next decade to meet this rapidly growing demand.

The world's demand for energy is also being fueled by the rapid rise in car ownership. Transportation already accounts for 30 percent of the world's energy use, mostly that created from oil. In India, the number of cars tripled between 1995 and 2005 and is expected to triple again by 2020. In Thailand and other Southeast Asian countries, the number of cars on the road is growing by 30 percent a year. Experts predict that within 20 years, developing nations will use half of all the oil produced worldwide.

As the demand for fossil fuels grows, concern also grows about their limited supply. Fossil fuels are a **nonrenewable resource**. That means that they cannot be replaced once they run out. Experts worry that the world has already used up a large portion of the existing oil supply. To meet these concerns, scientists are working to create new fuels that can provide clean and plentiful energy for the world's future.

chapter two

Fuels from Plants

As oil supplies decline, scientists hope to develop **renewable resources** that can take the place of fossil fuels. A renewable resource can be replaced after it is used; therefore there will always be enough of it to meet the world's needs. Many renewable resources are already in use as energy sources. Solar power, wind power, **hydroelectric power** from rivers, and nuclear power all provide renewable energy. However, issues of cost and safety along with environmental concerns, have prevented them from becoming more widely used. In addition, none of these energy sources is suitable for widespread use as a fuel for vehicles.

Biofuel Basics

Some of the most promising new sources of energy, especially for powering vehicles, are **biofuels**.

A test tube holds biofuel made from soybeans (shown in the background).

Biofuels are made from plants. Plants capture energy from the sun and store it in their tissues as chemicals called **hydrocarbons**. When the plants are used as fuel, these hydrocarbons release the stored energy. Fossil fuels also release energy through hydrocarbons. However, unlike the hydrocarbons in oil, coal, and natural gas, which took millions of years to form, plants can make hydrocarbons over just the few months it takes them to grow.

The energy stored in plants has been used as fuel for thousands of years, ever since humans discovered how to burn wood to create fires for cooking and keeping warm. Plants used to make biofuels, however, are not simply burned to create energy. Instead, biofuels are made by using chemicals to transform plant materials into liquid fuel that can be used in much the same way as gasoline or diesel fuel.

Biodiesel

There are two main types of biofuels: **biodiesel** and **ethanol**. Biodiesel is made from the vegetable oils found in plants such as seed from sunflowers, peanuts, and soybeans. Biodiesel can also be made

A technician checks the production of ethanol made from sugar cane.

from used cooking oil recycled from restaurants. Instead of being used as fuel by itself, biodiesel is usually mixed with regular diesel fuel made from petroleum. Therefore, biodiesel can be used only in diesel engines and not in gasoline engines. If the amount of biodiesel in the mix is small, the fuel can be used in any diesel engine. However, it is possible to run a vehicle on 100 percent, or pure, biodiesel if its engine is specially designed for that use.

Ethanol

Like biodiesel, ethanol is also made from plants. However, instead of being made from the oil-rich plants that produce biodiesel, ethanol is made from plants high in sugar, such as sugarcane, sugar beets, and corn. A process called fermentation changes the sugar in the plants into ethanol, a type of alcohol. Ethanol is mixed with unleaded gasoline for use in gasoline engines. The most common mixture is called E85—a blend of 85 percent ethanol and 15 percent gasoline. Cars and trucks with engines designed to run on E85 are called flexible-fuel vehicles. They can be powered by either ethanol or gasoline.

The Benefits of Biofuels

Running vehicles on biofuel can go a long way toward reducing the pollution created by cars and trucks. Compared to burning gasoline, burning ethanol pro-

A driver refuels her vehicle with fuel containing ethanol.

duces only half the amount of carbon dioxide. Vehicles that run on ethanol also produce less carbon monoxide and other polluting chemicals. Likewise, biodiesel is significantly less polluting than regular diesel fuel. When used at full strength, biodiesel produces 75 percent less carbon dioxide than diesel fuel. In addition, biodiesel exhaust contains almost none of the sulfur compounds that cause acid rain.

Besides creating less pollution, biofuels are much safer to transport than petroleum fuels. Biofuels are nontoxic and will easily break down in the environment if they are spilled onto the ground or in the water. Also, because they are made from plants, biofuels are a renewable source of energy. Therefore biofuels will always be available, even after all the world's fossil fuels are used up.

Another significant benefit to using biofuels is that they can be used in many engines. Engines not designed to use biofuels can usually be easily changed to accept them. In addition to powering vehicles, biofuels can power engines that produce electricity for factories or replace oil used for heating and cooking.

The Growing Use of Biofuels

Because they are easy to make and use and have many benefits to the environment, biofuels are

This ethanol production plant began operating in Colorado in 2006.

catching on quickly in many parts of the world. One of the first countries to invest large amounts of time and money into developing a biofuel industry was Brazil. Since 1975, Brazil has spent billions of dollars to develop a program to produce and use ethanol as a vehicle fuel. Brazil produces 3.5 billion gallons (13.2 billion liters) of ethanol a year, accounting for half of all the vehicle fuel in the country. Seven out of every ten cars sold in Brazil are flexible-fuel vehicles that can fill up at the country's twenty-nine thousand filling stations that carry ethanol. Brazil produces so much ethanol that it also exports the fuel for sale to other countries and plans to increase production to meet world demand.

Many other countries have followed Brazil's lead in producing biofuels. China recently built the world's largest ethanol producing facility. Thailand is building more than a dozen new ethanol factories. Biodiesel is also becoming widely used, especially in Europe where diesel cars that can readily burn the fuel are popular. More than fifty biodiesel facilities in Germany, France, Italy, and Spain produce more than 600 million gallons (2.2 billion liters) every year. South Africa, Australia, and Japan are also experimenting with alternatives to oil by both producing and importing biofuels.

While most biofuel is made from farm crops, the use of recycled vegetable oil for making biodiesel is also growing. In 2003, McDonald's restaurants in France began supplying used frying oil for recycling into biodiesel sold as heating oil. In Japan, a factory was specially built to recycle used cooking oil from KFC and other restaurants. A South African factory that makes biodiesel from cooking oil to power construction equipment cannot find enough used oil to meet its growing need.

Biofuels in the United States

Compared with many parts of the world, the United States has been slow to turn to biofuels as an alternative energy source. For example, Europe produces nearly twenty times as much biodiesel as the United States. During the 1980s and 1990s, only a few hundred gallons were produced each year in the United States, mostly through biofuel research. However, with rising oil prices and a declining oil supply, more attention is now being given to biofuels, especially ethanol.

In early 2006, President George W. Bush announced a plan to increase the United States' efforts to produce and use biofuels. This plan calls for doubling the current use of ethanol to 7.5 billion gallons (28 billion liters) by 2012. To meet this goal, there is a building boom underway for factories producing ethanol. In early 2006 there were ninety-two factories in operation and twenty-four more under construction. The automobile manufacturers Ford and General Motors also plan to increase their production of flexible-fuel vehicles able to operate on ethanol.

The use of biodiesel is growing in the United States as well. Many cities are switching their public transportation vehicles, school buses, and fire engines to biodiesel. Twenty national parks fuel their buses, construction equipment, and lawn mowers with biodiesel. Yosemite National Park in California even has its own mini-factory to convert used cooking oil from its restaurants into biodiesel for Park Service vehicles.

Yosemite National Park has turned to hybrid shuttles (pictured) to reduce pollution.

The use of biofuels in the United States and throughout the world is widely thought to be a positive way to decrease pollution and create a renewable source of energy. However, biofuels do have some drawbacks. Their use is likely only a partial solution to the world's demand for energy. In addition, biofuels may hold some new environmental challenges of their own.

chapter three

The Challenges of Biofuels

Because biodiesel and ethanol burn more cleanly than gasoline or diesel fuel, they create less pollution. Biofuels are also a renewable form of energy that will exist long after fossil fuels have been used up. Despite these benefits, however, some experts debate whether or not biofuels are really a long-term solution to the environmental problems caused by fossil fuels.

Do Biofuels Save Energy?

One point of disagreement is whether biofuels actually create more energy than is needed to produce them. Producing biofuels requires fuel, usually fossil fuels, to power tractors and other farm equipment to grow and harvest crops. Energy is also needed to power the factories that process the crops into biofuels. Researchers studying this issue have different opinions about the energy savings of biofuels. One study showed that it takes 29 percent more fossil fuel energy to produce ethanol from corn than the energy in the ethanol itself. Other studies show that biofuels provide more energy than it takes to produce them. Debate on this issue will likely continue.

Creating Fuel From Leftover Plant Matter

1. Extraneous parts of the corn plant, like leaves, husks and stems, are seperated from the harvested corn.
2. The material is chopped into small pieces and placed in an airtight gasifier tank.
3. With controlled temperature and oxygen content, biomass molecules break apart to produce a gas rich in carbon monoxide and hydrogen.
4. The hydrogen and carbon monoxide gas is used to replace natural gas to seperate steam to run both the gasifier and the ethanol plant.

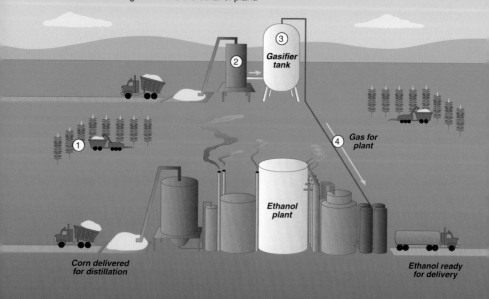

③ Gasifier tank

②

①

④ Gas for plant

Ethanol plant

Corn delivered for distillation

Ethanol ready for delivery

Source: *New York Times*

Creating Fuel From Farm Wastes

1. Silage, the residue left over from distilling corn into ethanol, is separated by centrifuge.
2. Some of the processed silage is fed to cattle, while some is pumped directly to the digester tank.
3. Manure from cattle is piped to the digester tank.
4. In the tank, the manure and the silage are digested by bacteria, producing methane gas.
5. The methane is used to replace natural gas in the distillation process.

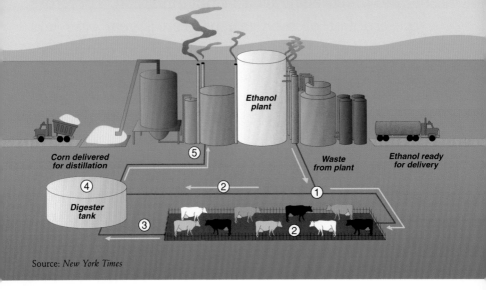

Source: *New York Times*

The Impact of Biofuels

In addition to the energy required to produce them, both biodiesel and ethanol still require the use of fossil fuels since they are typically mixed with regular gasoline and diesel fuel. Therefore, using biofuels will only stretch the supply of oil, not replace it completely. Eventually, when fossil fuels run out, it will be impossible to create biofuels in any mixture less than a 100 percent strength.

Additionally, although interest in biofuels is growing, they are currently used in such small amounts that they have little overall impact on fossil fuel use worldwide. For example, in 2005 the

United States produced 75 million gallons (284 million liters) of biodiesel. But the total amount of regular diesel fuel used each day in the United States is 136 million gallons (515 million liters). Therefore the amount of biodiesel used in a year was less than even a day's worth of the oil consumed. Likewise, the 1.2 billion gallons (4.5 billion liters) of biodiesel used in Europe in 2006 was only a small fraction of the total 88 trillion gallons (333 trillion liters) of diesel fuel consumed.

Ethanol production in the United States is significantly higher than that of biodiesel. A total of 3.9 billion gallons (14.8 billion liters) of ethanol was produced in 2005. However, the United States uses 390 million gallons (1.5 billion liters) of gasoline each day. Therefore, the amount of ethanol cur-

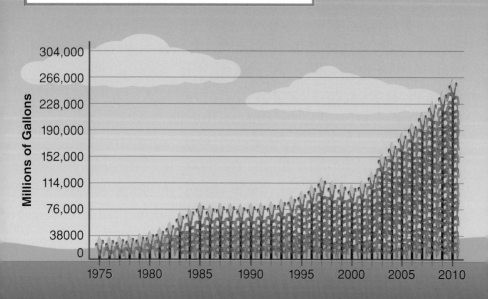

World Ethanol Production

Millions of Gallons

rently used each year replaces only a ten-day supply of gas.

The Biofuel Supply

Several factors stand in the way of biofuels becoming more widely used and having a greater impact on reducing the use of fossil fuels. One factor is cost. Biofuels usually cost more to produce than regular gas or diesel. To encourage the use of biofuels, governments pay farmers for some of the cost of growing biofuel crops. They also pay part of the construction costs for new biofuel factories. This government support keeps the price of biofuels similar to that of petroleum fuels. However, this support will not continue

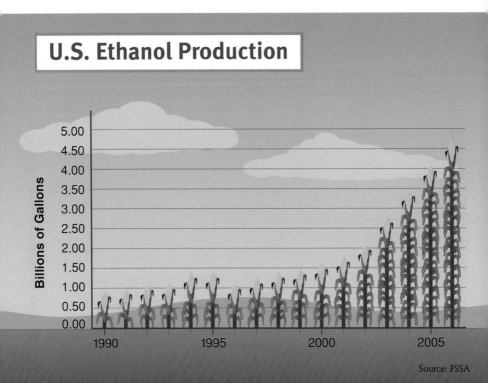

U.S. Ethanol Production

Source: FSSA

forever. Without it, the price of biofuels will likely grow much higher.

Another problem is that there are not many places for the general public to buy biofuels. Companies and governments using biofuels usually have fueling stations for supplying their vehicle fleets. However, although as many as 5 million private vehicles in the United States can run on biodiesel or ethanol, few filling stations carry these fuels. In fact, there are only 600 public E85 fueling stations in thirty states, mostly in the Midwest. California, the state with the highest proportion of the nation's cars, has only one. The number of ethanol fueling locations is expected to quadruple in 2006, but even so that will make it available in only a fraction of the country's 170,000 stations. It will take many years—perhaps decades—for biofuels to be widely available to fuel millions of vehicles.

Growing Biofuel Crops

Another factor that limits the growth of the biofuel industry is the amount of plant material available to produce biofuels. It takes a great deal of land to grow biofuel crops. In fact, it is thought that there is not enough cropland worldwide to produce the amount of biofuel needed to replace fossil fuels completely. For example, for the United States to replace just 10 percent of the fuel used in transportation with biofuels would require 40 percent of available cropland. Using this much agricultural land for biofuels could decrease the amount of food crops produced, thereby increasing food costs.

Some crops provide more biofuels than others. If all the corn grown in the United States were used to make ethanol, it would replace only a fourth of U.S. fuel needs. Crops with higher sugar content, however, such as sugar cane, can produce more biofuel using less farmland. Sugar-rich crops

Sugar cane is washed before it can be made into ethanol.

grow best in warmer climates with a year-round growing season, such as those in Southeast Asia, Australia, and central South America. Sugarcane grown in these places can produce five times more biofuel from each acre of farmland compared to the corn grown in the United States and Europe. As a result, many countries in these regions are rapidly developing programs to produce biofuels both for use at home and to sell to countries with poorer growing climates.

Biofuel Crops and the Environment

Growing biofuel crops may appear to be an environmentally friendly way to reduce the use of fossil fuels. However, concerns are growing about the environmental risks of increasing agriculture to make biofuels. In addition to energy, farming requires the use of large amounts of water, chemical fertilizers, and toxic pesticides to produce crops. All of these practices can harm the environment.

Another concern is the rate at which some countries are clearing land to create new farmland for producing biofuel crops. Several countries in Southeast Asia have announced plans to create large palm oil plantations to supply the growing demand for biodiesel. Palm oil can be used for making biodiesel. This crop can be grown at very low cost in the tropics, providing great profit to companies and governments selling it as a source of fuel.

Creating palm oil plantations causes severe damage to tropical rain forest environments, however. Rain forests are home to more species of plants and animals than any other habitat. When

A worker on a palm plantation piles up the oily palm fruit for processing into biodiesel fuel.

this habitat is destroyed to make way for planting palm trees, countless plants and animals disappear.

On the islands of Sumatra and Borneo, 9.8 million acres (4 million hectares) of forest have been cleared for growing oil palms, with many more acres targeted for clearing in the near future. In 2006, the government of Indonesia announced a plan to create the world's largest palm oil plantation on Borneo. This enormous plantation, covering 4.4 million acres (1.8 million hectares), will permanently destroy habitat that is home to endangered species such as orangutans, rhinos, tigers, and gibbons.

These environmental concerns about biodiesel production add to the debate about the long-term potential biofuels have for reducing the need for fossil fuels. Some researchers believe that instead of being the solution themselves, biofuels are only a bridge to other solutions to meeting the world's demand for energy.

chapter Four

The Future of Biofuels

As consumers learn to accept biofuels, demand for them will continue to rise. Meeting this growing demand will require the development of an entire biofuel industry similar to the oil industry. Private companies, governments, and equipment manufacturers will need to work together to build a network for growing biofuel crops, building and operating biofuel factories, and distributing biofuels to consumers.

New Sources of Biofuels

Because the amount of farmland available for growing biofuel crops is limited, researchers are exploring ways that crops can produce more biofuel without using more land. A new generation of

Sunflower plantations like this one in northern India may soon provide biofuel as well as food.

biofuels is being developed for this purpose. In the past, only the plant parts containing sugar and oil could be used to make biofuel. New technology, however, allows biofuel to be made from the plant's cellulose instead. Cellulose is the stiff material that makes up most of a plant.

The key to this new process was the discovery of a fungus from the jungles of Asia. This fungus grows on items made from natural fibers, such as canvas tents and clothes, causing them to break down, or rot. A researcher studying this process of "jungle rot" discovered that the fungus produces a special chemical called an enzyme. The enzyme quickly breaks the cloth down into sugars that the fungus can feed upon.

Researchers are now able to produce this enzyme in the laboratory and use it to transform almost any part of a plant into sugar. This sugar can then be fermented into ethanol, in this case a type called **cellulosic ethanol**. This process allows biofuel producers to use plant parts that were once considered waste, such as cornstalks and leaves. More importantly, this process allows a whole new range of crops to be used to make ethanol.

Instead of being grown for sugar or oil content, plants used for cellulosic ethanol are grown to get as much plant mass as possible. Therefore, researchers are focusing on developing plants that grow to a large size quickly. These plants include willow and poplar trees, sunflowers with fifty seed heads each, and grasses such as wheat and oats. When harvested, these plants are chopped up and treated with enzymes to produce ethanol.

Reducing the Costs

This new process allows larger amounts of biofuel to be produced from each acre of land. This will help reduce the cost of biofuels, the energy required for farming, and pesticide and fertilizer use. It will also reduce the need for new land to be cleared for farming. This is an advantage for smaller countries that have limited amounts of farmland. It also benefits countries in more northerly climates since they can use crops better suited for growing in their region. According to a study by the U.S. Department of Energy, cellulosic ethanol could replace up to 30 percent of the country's gasoline use by 2030 without affecting the food supply.

Biogas

Another type of biofuel receiving attention from researchers is **biogas**. Biogas is made mostly of a gas called **methane**. Methane is produced when microscopic animals known as bacteria digest plant food. One common place to find these bacteria is in cow manure. Normally, the methane from bacteria in cow manure is released into the atmosphere. However, a simple system called a digester can capture the methane to use as an energy source instead.

Methane can be used for energy on both a small and a large scale. In many developing countries in Asia and Africa, for example, households have small digesters fed by the manure from just a few cows. The methane collected is piped into homes for cooking.

Dairy farms use the same process on a much larger scale, collecting methane from the manure produced by hundreds or thousands of cows. This biogas is usually used to power equipment to operate the dairy. However, new uses for biogas are being found off the farm. In 2005, the world's first biogas-

Women in the Republic of Georgia tend a backyard tank that turns cow manure into methane fuel for home use.

powered train began making daily trips in Sweden, replacing a train powered by a diesel engine.

Methane Fuel Cells

Researchers have also begun experimenting with methane from cow manure to power energy-producing **fuel cells**. Fuel cells use the hydrogen gas found in methane to create and store electricity, much like a battery. If experiments with methane-powered fuel cells are successful, they could have widespread use. Methane could be collected from other places where it is produced by bacteria in decaying waste, such as sewage treatment plants and landfills.

In fact, one of the first fuel cells to make electricity from waste biogas was at the wastewater treatment plant in Portland, Oregon. Installed at a cost of $1.3 million, the fuel cell produces enough electricity to save the city of Portland $60,000 a year in energy costs. Collecting the biogas also pays off by reducing the environmental impact of the treatment plant. Methane is a greenhouse gas and contributes to global warming if allowed to escape into the atmosphere.

Fuel cells such as Portland's are considered by many experts to be the most promising solution for creating energy in the future. Fuel cells are an extremely clean power source; they produce no pollution. They are still very costly, however. So for now, fuel cells are still mostly experimental.

A Bridge to the Future?

Despite recent advances in fuel cells and biofuels, no one can predict what the future of energy will hold. Current thought is that the use of biogas, biodiesel, and ethanol is simply a step in the direction of becoming less dependent on fossil fuels. Used with other alternative forms of energy, such as solar and wind power, biofuels may allow the world to stretch fossil fuel supplies a little longer. However, future research may lead to biofuels that can completely replace petroleum, or scientists may discover an entirely new solution.

Learning to Conserve

In the meantime, almost everyone agrees that people could go much further in conserving the fossil fuels that remain. Most people, especially in the

Still in the experimental stage, fuel cells like this one offer promise for the future.

Wind turbines, like biofuels, are an important alternative to fossil fuels.

United States, give little thought to how much energy they use every day. Many energy-saving actions, such as driving in carpools or wearing a sweater instead of turning up the heat, require little personal sacrifice. If millions of people adopted such actions, it would make a huge dent in the amount of fossil fuels used and pollution created. This would allow both people and the environment to move more smoothly into an uncertain energy future.

Glossary

acid rain: Rain containing acid formed in the atmosphere by the burning of fossil fuels. The toxic acid falling in this rain harms and kills plants and wildlife.

biodiesel: Fuel made from the vegetable oils found in plant seed such as from sunflowers, peanuts, and soybeans.

biofuels: Fuels made from the energy stored in the tissues of plants.

biogas: A mixture of methane and carbon dioxide produced when bacteria break down organic matter.

cellulosic ethanol: An alcohol fuel made from the starchy parts of plants.

ethanol: An alcohol fuel made from the sugars in plants.

fossil fuels: The remains of plants and animals, transformed by great heat and pressure over millions of years into oil, coal, and natural gas used as energy sources.

fuel cells: Devices that use a chemical reaction to convert fuel to electricity.

global warming: An increase in the average temperature of the earth's atmosphere.

greenhouse gases: Gases in the atmosphere that trap some of the heat radiating from the earth's surface.

hydrocarbons: Chemicals in the tissues of plants that store energy from the sun.

hydroelectric power: Electricity produced by flowing water.

methane: A gas produced by the breakdown of plant matter by bacteria.

nonrenewable resource: A natural resource from the earth that is limited in supply and cannot be replaced when it is used up.

renewable resources: Natural resources that can be replaced over time.

For Further Exploration

Books

Rob Bowden, *Energy*. San Diego, CA: KidHaven 2004. This easy-to-understand book discusses concerns about limited sources of energy such as coal and oil. It also examines many alternative, renewable energy sources being used around the world.

Kris Hirschmann, *Pollution*. Detroit: KidHaven 2005. This book examines the steps taken to decrease pollution caused by cars and other sources.

Kimberly M. Miller, *What If We Run Out of Fossil Fuels?* New York: Children's Press, 2002. This book examines what life would be like without cars or other modern machines fueled by oil. The author also looks at alternative energy sources to prepare for a future without fossil fuels.

Sally Morgan, *Alternative Energy Sources*. Chicago: Heinemann Library, 2003. An overview of different options for replacing fossil fuels. The author examines the pros and cons of using various alternative energy sources such as water power, solar power, and biofuels.

Web Sites

Energy Information Administration, Energy Kid's Page (www.eia.doe.gov/kids/). This United States government site offers a wide variety of energy-related information designed for kids. It includes information on the history and uses of energy as well as descriptions of both renewable and nonrenewable energy sources.

Environmental Literacy Council (www.enviro literacy.org). The Environmental Literacy Council is dedicated to helping students understand environmental issues. Its Web site contains resources on almost every aspect of the natural world, including detailed information on energy issues.

Union of Concerned Scientists, Renewable Energy Basics (www.ucsusa.org/clean_energy/renewable_energy_basics/). This site describes different renewable energy sources, including biofuels, as well as the environmental issues surrounding energy use.

United States Environmental Protection Agency, Mobile Source Emissions—Past Present and Future (www.epa.gov/otaq/invntory/overview/pollutants/). This government site provides detailed information on the different types of pollution caused by cars, including gases such as carbon monoxide and carbon dioxide.

Index

About the Author

Karen D. Povey has spent her career as a conservation educator, working to instill in people of all ages an appreciation for wildlife and wild places. Karen makes her home in Tacoma, Washington, where she presents live animal education programs at Point Defiance Zoo & Aquarium. She has written many books on wildlife and the environment, including *The Leopard, The Condor, Life in a Swamp,* and *Hybrid Cars.*